SHOPPING

GW00854083

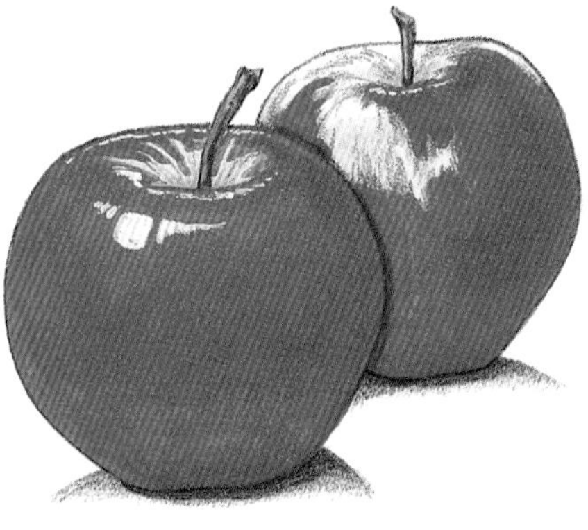

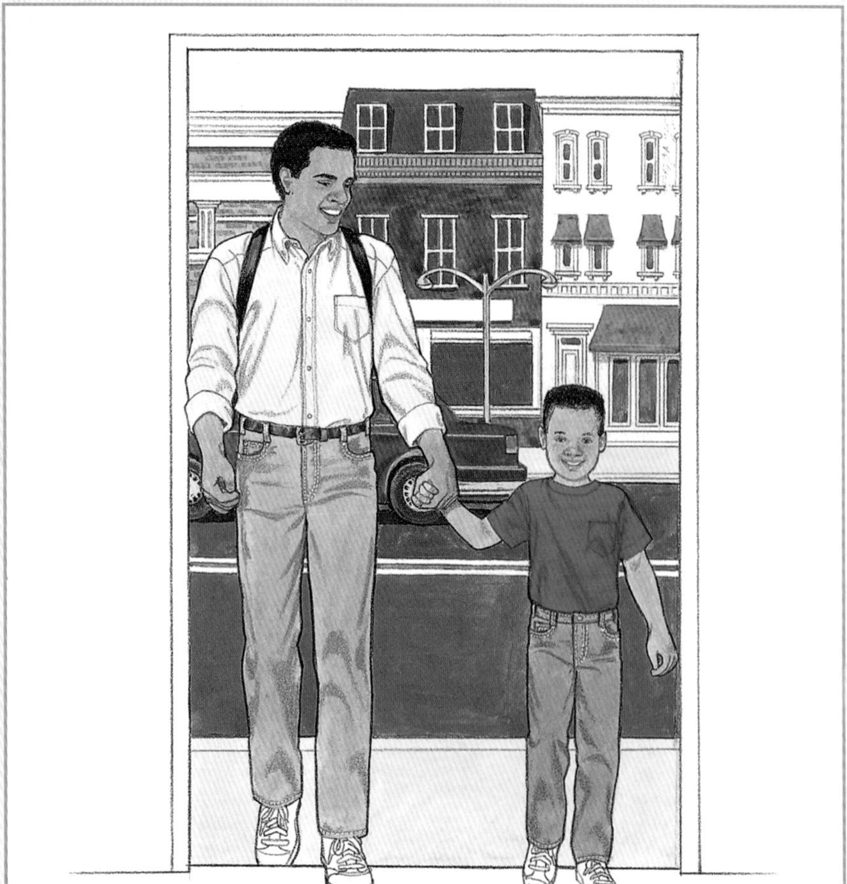

Dad and I went shopping.

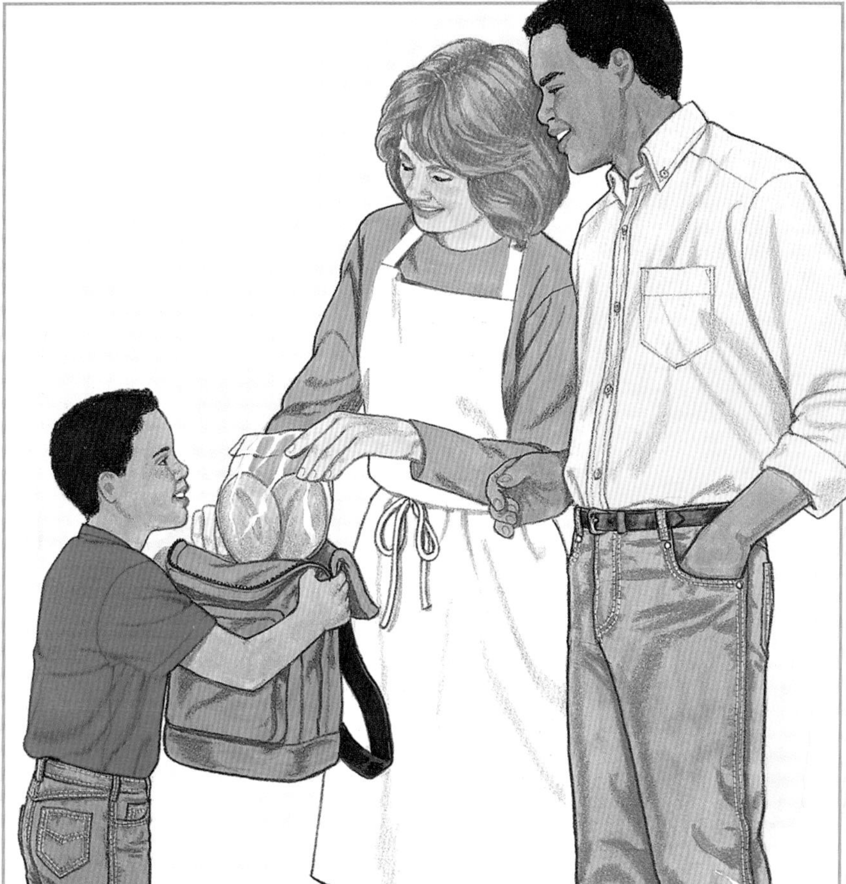

We bought some bread rolls,

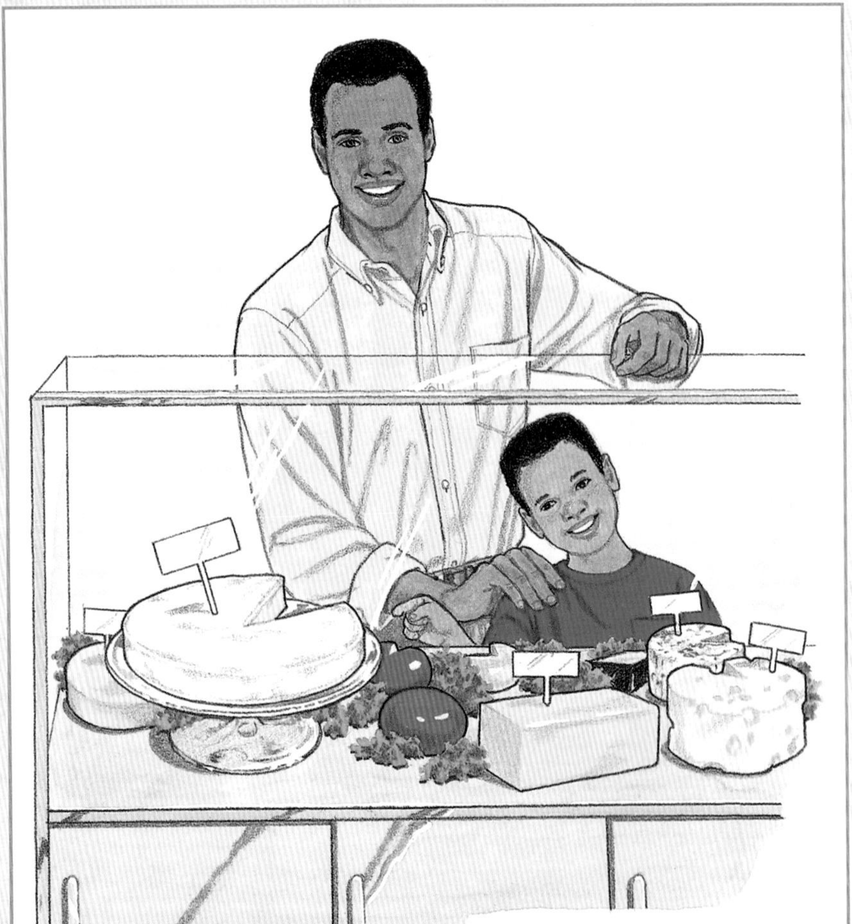

some cheese,

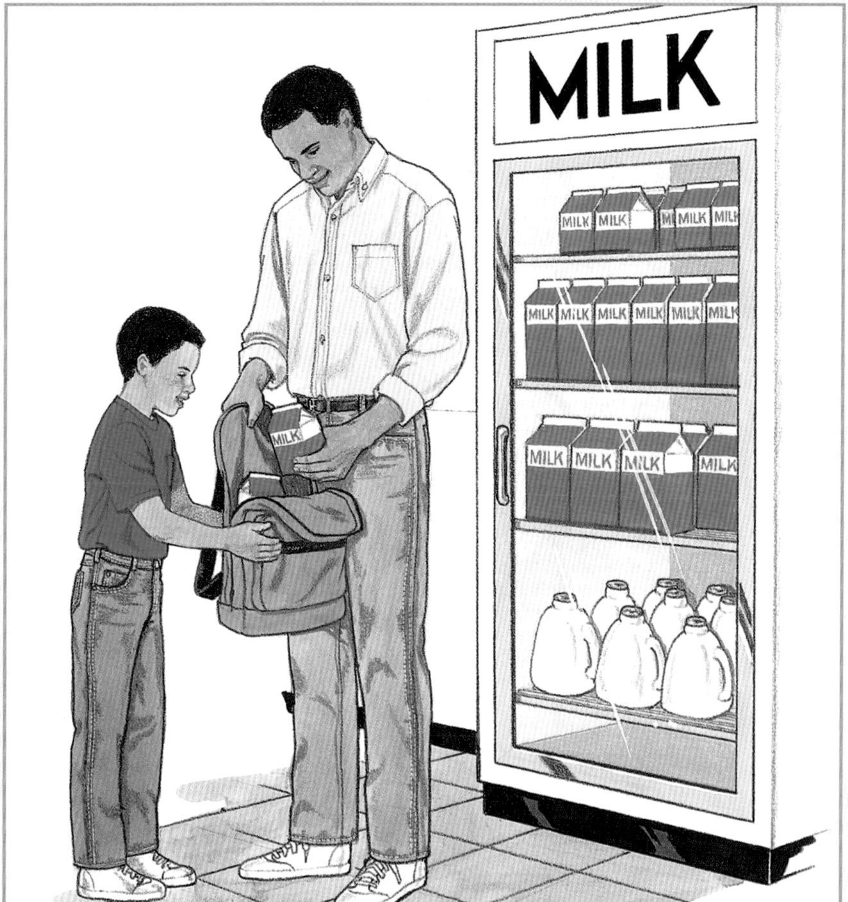

some milk,

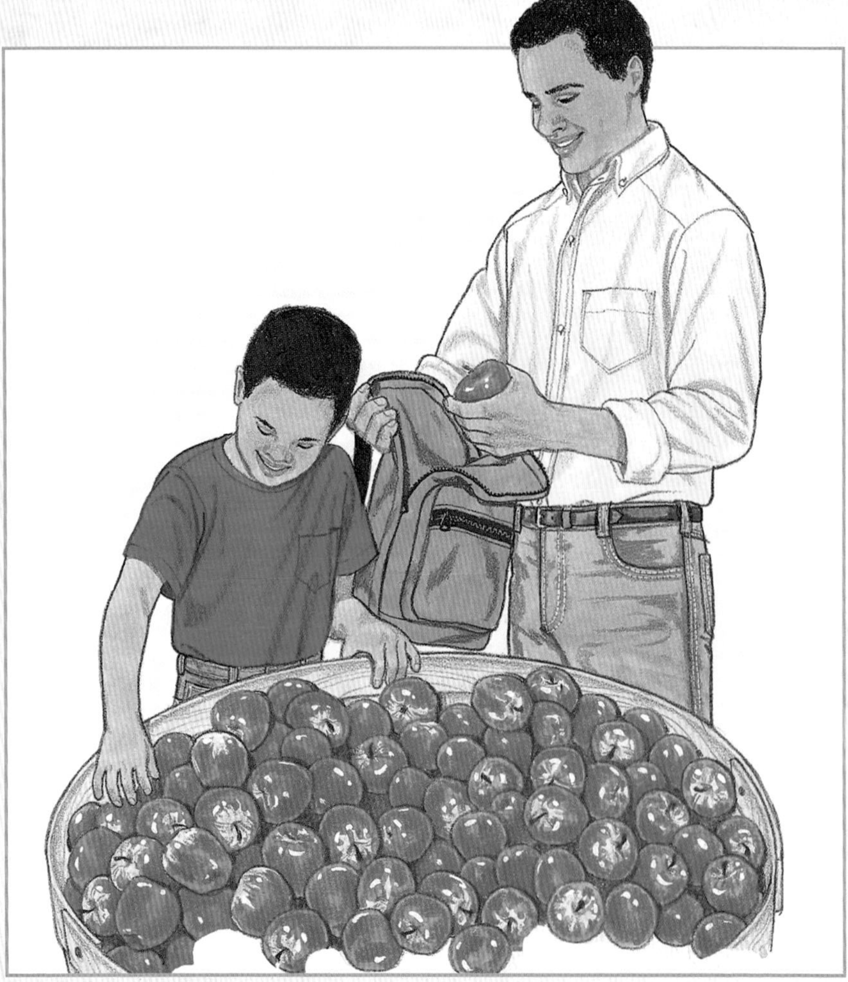

and some apples.

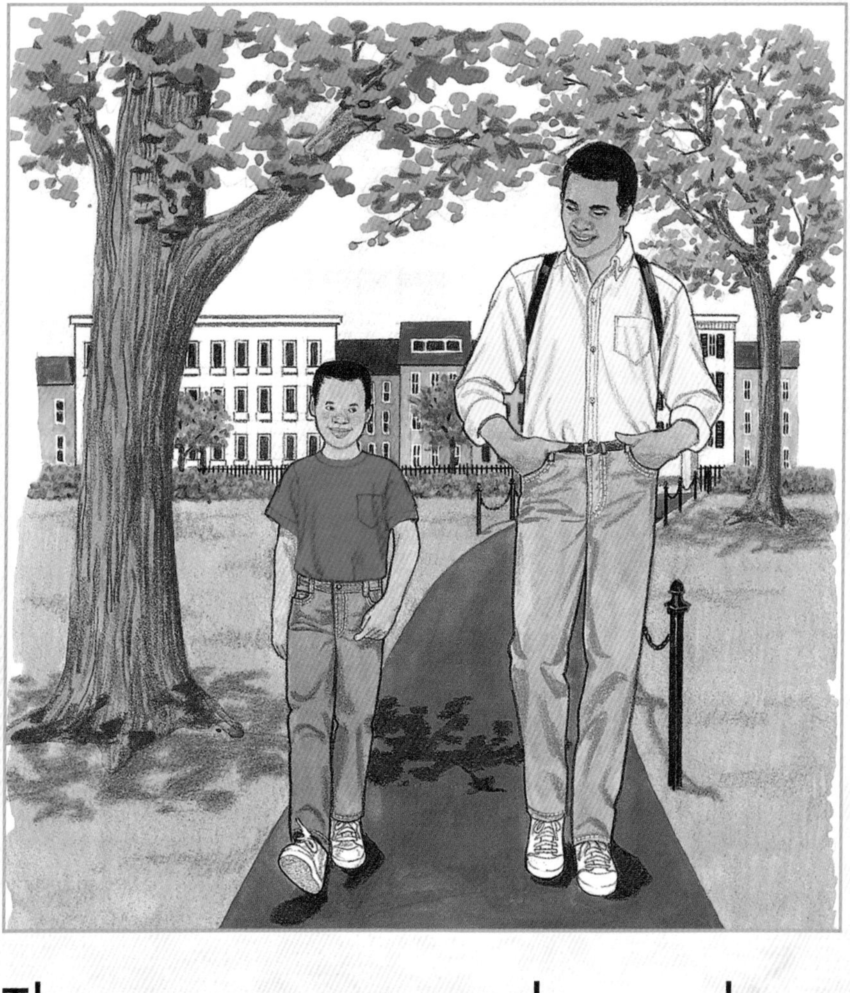

Then we went to the park ...

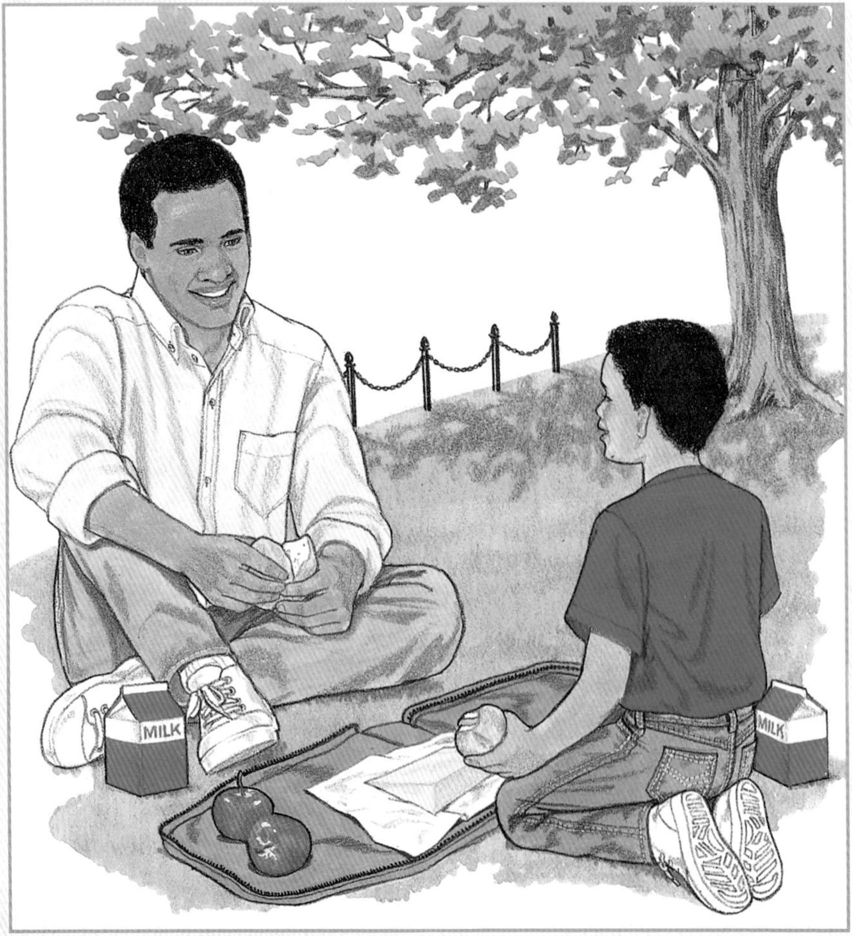

and had lunch.